Leaving

A Play

Don Woods

A Samuel French Acting Edition

SAMUELFRENCH-LONDON.CO.UK
SAMUELFRENCH.COM

Copyright © 1989 by Samuel French Ltd
All Rights Reserved

LEAVING is fully protected under the copyright laws of the British Commonwealth, including Canada, the United States of America, and all other countries of the Copyright Union. All rights, including professional and amateur stage productions, recitation, lecturing, public reading, motion picture, radio broadcasting, television and the rights of translation into foreign languages are strictly reserved.

ISBN 978-0-573-13264-3

www.samuelfrench-london.co.uk

www.samuelfrench.com

FOR AMATEUR PRODUCTION ENQUIRIES

UNITED KINGDOM AND WORLD
EXCLUDING NORTH AMERICA
plays@SamuelFrench-London.co.uk
020 7255 4302/01

Each title is subject to availability from Samuel French,

depending upon country of performance.

CAUTION: Professional and amateur producers are hereby warned that *LEAVING* is subject to a licensing fee. Publication of this play does not imply availability for performance. Both amateurs and professionals considering a production are strongly advised to apply to the appropriate agent before starting rehearsals, advertising, or booking a theatre. A licensing fee must be paid whether the title is presented for charity or gain and whether or not admission is charged.

The professional rights in this play are controlled by Samuel French Ltd, 52 Fitzroy Street, London, W1T 5JR.

No one shall make any changes in this title for the purpose of production. No part of this book may be reproduced, stored in a retrieval system, or transmitted in any form, by any means, now known or yet to be invented, including mechanical, electronic, photocopying, recording, videotaping, or otherwise, without the prior written permission of the publisher. No one shall upload this title, or part of this title, to any social media websites.

The right of Don Woods to be identified as author of this work has been asserted by him in accordance with Section 77 of the Copyright, Designs and Patents Act 1988

CHARACTERS

Auntie
Lil
Daisy

The action of the play takes place in a room in a suburban house

Time — the present

LEAVING

The back room of a semi-detached house on a suburban estate. An early evening in August

The basic set consists of a carpet, a sofa and a coffee table. DL *is an armchair and* DR, *a sideboard. Slightly* US *and to one side of the sofa is an ironing-board on which is an iron. A telephone and a stack of mail can be seen on the sideboard. The set can, of course, be augmented with the furniture and dressing typical of that found in the back room of a semi-detached house on a suburban estate. A mirror is also required on the set. If there is a flat behind the sideboard it can be hung on it—otherwise it can be free-standing on the sideboard. The* CURTAIN *rises to reveal Auntie ironing one of Bill's shirts. She is in her early eighties and wears a comfortable dressing-gown and slippers. She takes a cigarette out of her mouth, stubs it in an ash-tray, leans over for her glass and takes a large gulp of gin and tonic. She finishes ironing the shirt, places it on a stack of clothes and takes them to the kitchen*

The front door is heard to open and Lil enters the room. She is aged about forty but, in reality, she looks much younger and very attractive. She wears a light summer coat under which is a stylish dress. Carrying a small suitcase, she walks slowly DSC *and looks around the room with a sad, melancholic expression*

Auntie returns with more damp clothes. Seeing Lil's back and thinking that a stranger has entered the room, she places the clothes on the ironing-board and angrily crosses to her

Auntie (*sharply*) Excuse me! Would you mind telling me what you are ...

Lil turns to face her and Auntie gasps in surprise. She is not sure who she is looking at

(*Bewildered*) Who ...? Who ...?
Lil (*quietly*) Hello, Auntie.
Auntie (*perplexed*) It's not ... It can't be ... (*She moves a step closer*) Who ...?

Lil It's me.
Auntie (*whispering*) Lil?
Lil (*quietly*) Yes.
Auntie Is it you—Lil?
Lil Yes, Auntie—it's me.
Auntie (*devastated*) But ... your *face*. Oh God! Oh my God! What ... ? What have you done to your face?
Lil I didn't do anything to it. As a matter of fact, it was done for me.
Auntie (*about to cry*) But—Lil! (*Pause*) In the name of God what have you done to your face—your nose?
Lil Nice isn't it? (*She places the suitcase at the side of the sofa*)
Auntie Oh no! (*Sobbing*) Oh God, no.
Lil Auntie, will you stop all the "Oh Godding" and turn off those silly tears. I've had enough of my *own* these last few weeks.
Auntie I can't help it. I'm too old for shocks like this. I can't cope with any more shocks.

Lil takes off her coat and throws it over the back of the armchair

Lil You can cope. (*Wearily*) You can cope.
Auntie But Lil. Tell me—(*sadly*) what have you done?

Lil goes to the sideboard. She picks up the mail and returns with it to the sofa

Lil Something I should have done years ago but never had the courage to—or the money.
Auntie But ...
Lil (*abruptly*) When did you get back?
Auntie (*unnerved by the question*) This morning.
Lil Why?
Auntie Lil, tell me what you've done.
Lil (*thoughtfully*) What I've done. (*Pause*) I've been away. (*She sorts out the mail*)
Auntie Where?
Lil To a hospital—in London.
Auntie What for?
Lil It's simple enough, but like so many of the so-called simple things in my life, it would take too long to explain. (*Pause; sharply*) Why did you come back?
Auntie What sort of hospital?

Lil A private one.
Auntie And you let them mess about with your face?
Lil Why not? They couldn't have made it any worse.
Auntie But what did they do?
Lil In layman's terms they cut around the inside of my nostrils, pulled back the skin and sawed off the end of my nose. Incidentally, they prefer to call it plastic surgery, not messing about. But in my case it probably amounts to the same thing.
Auntie But why, Lil?
Lil As I said, it would take too long to explain. (*Curtly*) Is this all the mail?
Auntie Yes.
Lil Any horror stories?
Auntie No. It's mainly statements for settled accounts.
Lil Good. I hoped it would be.
Auntie And when did all this happen?
Lil What? Me settling the bills?
Auntie (*impatiently*) No. That on your face.
Lil My little op'? About seven weeks ago.
Auntie Tell me Lil, honestly, why did you do it?
Lil (*laughing out loud*) Oh, Auntie!
Auntie But...
Lil You honestly don't expect me to answer that. Don't pretend to be so naïve.
Auntie But Lil—you've ruined your face.
Lil It's all aesthetics, isn't it? (*She continues to sort the mail into separate piles*)
Auntie Did you pay?
Lil (*laughing ruefully*) Did I pay!
Auntie How?
Lil Through the nose, if you'll forgive the pun.
Auntie (*hand to mouth with shock*) Oooo! And that dress... and the shoes... where did you get money like that from?
Lil D'you like them?
Auntie No—I don't. They're common.
Lil There's no-one like good old Auntie for making me feel better.
Auntie Tell me, Lil, where did you get the money from?
Lil I had a sale.
Auntie Of what?
Lil Everything I could lay my hands on.

Auntie From here?

Lil Hmm. Where else?

Auntie I wondered why the house looked bare.

Lil Yes, different isn't it. All that's left are the bare essentials—the stuff that no-one wanted. It's all gone. Auntie. His clothes, his junk, even his old car. Even mother's jewellery.

Auntie (*shocked*) Oh Lil, you haven't sold your mother's jewellery?

Lil I certainly did.

Auntie (*very upset*) Your mother's jewellery!

Lil Hmm. Why not? She can't wear it—she's been dead seventeen years.

Auntie Not all of it, surely?

Lil All of it.

Auntie Not her wedding ring, I hope.

Lil Hmm. That was the first to go. A repulsive little man smelling of sweat came round and literally pounced on it. Gave me quite a good price.

Auntie Oh Lil—how could you do such a thing?

Lil With the greatest of ease. I made a quick telephone call and there he was—the repulsive little man—grabbing the lot.

Auntie You didn't let the brooches go, did you?

Lil The brooches, the ear-rings, even the lockets containing her hair. Oh, and her gold-rimmed glasses as well.

Auntie (*going to the ironing-board*) I never thought I would live to see the day—never. What came over you? Have you gone insane?

Lil goes to the sideboard. She throws the mail on to it and turns

Lil (*raising her voice*) Auntie—have you gone so senile that you can't remember what happened here eight weeks ago?

There is no reply

Well come on, Auntie, answer me.

Auntie starts to iron

Auntie Oh not now, Lil, I'm too upset for all that.

Lil You seem to have conveniently forgotten that eight weeks ago Bill ran off with a slut called Daisy Parsons and I was left here with three thousand pounds worth of debt.

Leaving

Auntie Of course I remember.

Lil Then you will also recall that two days later, when I was seriously contemplating suicide, *you* left.

Auntie I explained it all in the note.

Lil Oh yes—the mysterious note. The one in which you said your sister, Milly, was seriously ill and that, you, of all people, had been asked to go down to Kent and look after her for the rest of her life.

There is no reply

I was on my own, Auntie, and I did what I did because I had no bloody alternative. Which brings me back to Milly.

Auntie I think I'll put the kettle on. I'm dying for a cup of tea.

Lil What's wrong with the gin? Isn't it wet enough?

Auntie That's the first drink I've had since this morning.

Lil (*pointedly*) Tell me about Milly.

Auntie (*about to leave*) All that ironing has made me as dry as a bone.

Lil (*shouting*) Auntie!

Auntie (*turning; ruffled*) What?

Lil Tell me about Milly. What happened? Did Basil throw you out?

Auntie Lil, you're not the only one who's been upset. And I'm too ill and tired to take part in a post mortem. D'you know you've really made me depressed today. Depressed and frightened.

Lil (*giving up*) What's the point.

Lil goes to the sofa. She picks up her case and takes it back to the sideboard

Auntie Doing what you did. There was no need for it. And having all that done to your face. I feel like vomitting.

Lil You'll get used to it—I have—almost.

Auntie It was all so unnecessary. You were perfectly all right as you were. You had a good nose. Aristocratic looking. Perhaps it was a little on the large size but who ... ?

Lil It was grotesque and hideous and you know it.

Auntie It wasn't.

Lil I was sick of being stared at and laughed at. Sick of people looking at me with their eyes transfixed on it.

Auntie It was all in your mind.

Lil How d'you know what was in my mind? It wasn't stuck in the middle of *your* face. I looked like a freak—I was a freak. Like something out of a circus.
Auntie It wasn't that bad.
Lil I couldn't even walk past a bus queue without getting sniggers. And those names—how I hated them.
Auntie But it never really bothered you.
Lil Maybe not on the outside. But on the inside—it was one lone cry of anguish—one long shriek of pain.
Auntie But you were always in the public eye. All these years you've been in the drama group. You love being on stage.
Lil It's different then. On stage I become someone else. I can forget who I am. Anyway, it's all over now. I shan't go there again. I have a new drama ahead of me—living. (*She opens the sideboard drawer, selects certain papers and items and places them in the suitcase*)
Auntie (*shocked*) You're not thinking of . . . ?
Lil I don't need it any more.
Auntie (*sadly—almost pleading*) Oh Lil, you're not giving up your drama group, surely?
Lil (*shivering*) It's cold in here. Why is it so cold?
Auntie I was frightened to turn on the central heating because of the bills. (*Pause*) Tell me Lil, you're not going to pack in your drama group, are you? It's the only thing you've got in your life.
Lil It *was* the only thing I had in my life. (*Pause*) I had an audience with Muriel the week you both left.
Auntie That old cow.
Lil Isn't she? Lionel has now retired and because of her years of devoted service to the group, they've elected her head of the Casting Committee.
Auntie Devoted service! That group survived *despite* her, not *because* of her.
Lil I had a thundering row with her. You remember last March when they promised me the lead in the next production?
Auntie Yes. You always wanted to play that part.
Lil Well, I'm not.
Auntie Go on. What is she up to?
Lil Well, she started with her usual song and dance routine about having the interests of the group at heart and how she'd agonized over my suitability for the role. In her honest and

unbiased opinion, I was too old and too ugly to be cast. And if I were, I would turn the society into a laughing stock.

Auntie The cheeky bitch!

Lil She'd called a special meeting of the committee and they gave the part to, surprise, surprise, sweet little Eileen.

Auntie Her daughter?

Lil There's only one Eileen in the society.

Auntie But that insufferable little madam can't act. She can't act, she can't sing, she can't dance and she's blind in one eye. (*Angrily*) She is completely devoid of *all* human talent.

Lil *But*—she's Muriel's daughter.

Auntie But that's criminal. I hope you gave her a flea in her ear.

Lil You can't reason with a person like Muriel. But we had a monumental row. It was quite degrading.

Auntie But it's a fix. She mustn't be allowed to get away with it.

Lil It was quite funny, now that I think of it. She started to scream at me and for the first time in my life, I screamed back. (*Pause*) She was horribly offensive. She asked how a woman who looked like Cyrano de Bergerac could possibly play Joan of Arc.

Auntie You should have slapped her across the face.

Lil Why? She was right. Callous—but right. Let's face it, I looked like a Pinocchio clone.

Auntie She wasn't right.

Lil They used me, you see. All those years ... playing Widow Twankey parts or the Ugly Sister ... or the witch with her cauldron. All that effort ... and for what?

Auntie But Lil ... (*Pause*) But—you have talent—you can act—they can't. Don't let her stop you now. (*Angrily*) Ohhh! D'you know, I've a good mind to ring her and give her a piece of my mind.

Lil Why? She did me a favour.

Auntie A favour! Muriel Evans never, ever, does anyone any favours. And that goes for the rest of them. I was only thinking about them the other day. Have you noticed whenever the phone rings it's always somebody wanting something? Think of it—whenever this phone goes it is *always* somebody wanting something. It's never anyone wanting to do something for us or give us something. No. It's always someone wanting something. So don't talk about favours. You can't turn the other cheek all your life. Look at them for what they are and tell them so.

Lil I did. Anyway, I'm grateful to her. After she'd left I cried for hours. Then it all turned to anger. (*Pause*) Then I looked in the mirror and my anger turned to hope. That obscene woman had unwittingly given me the impetus I'd sought all my life. (*Pause*) And in a split second I knew that my life would never be the same again. For better or worse, I didn't give a damn.

Auntie So it was she who made you mutilate your face.

Lil But you will agree, Auntie, this Pinocchio clone looks different. (*Hurt*) Come on, Auntie, give me a bit of encouragement. Tell me how nice I look.

Auntie I can't. You look hard ... and common. It's unnatural what you've done. It's not right to change what God gave you. And you can't escape the past. So why try?

Lil God? Funny isn't it how people take to thinking of God when they become geriatric? Since when have you been religious?

Auntie I don't believe in religion but I believe in God. You sold everything this family held dear so you could look like a woman of easy virtue. It's a disgrace. (*She walks to the ironing-board and starts to iron a shirt*)

Lil (*watching her for a while*) Why are you doing that?

Auntie The ironing? I always do the ironing.

Lil Those days are over, Auntie. Don't you understand?

Auntie I'll go and make the tea. If I don't get a drink soon I'll drop. (*She walks towards the kitchen*)

Lil What makes you think you can suddenly show up, do a bit of ironing and everything will be the same?

Auntie What are you talking about?

Lil You left me, Auntie. Don't you remember?

Auntie (*uneasily*) Lil, I ... I didn't *leave* you.

Lil You didn't?

Auntie Lil, she's my sister. She was very ill and she needed me for a while.

Lil That's not the way your note read.

Auntie (*angrily*) It *is*.

Lil Shall I read it to you?

Auntie Oh, let's not go through all that. You knew what I meant. I was upset and all of a dither.

Lil What happened? Did Basil throw you out?

Auntie No. No. It wasn't like that. Oh Lil—shut up.

Lil I sat here that day for eight hours in the cold, watching the rain run down the window. I was surrounded by unpaid bills and final demands and I was worried sick you might have had an accident. Then I saw your little note, partly concealed behind the clock. And those words will remain in my brain for as long as I live. Especially the bit about "Forgive me but at my age I have to think of myself because no-one else will".

Auntie (*sobbing*) Oh Lil, you don't understand what I'd been through. I was worried and ill. Bill had gone and you had all those debts. You don't realize how insecure you feel when you get to my age. (*Pause*) I've always had this terrible dread of ending up in a home.

Lil Why? I've looked after your every need for a quarter of a century. I've devoted a large part of my life to seeing that you wanted for nothing. Why should I suddenly become inhuman and throw you into a home?

Auntie I just didn't know what was to become of us. All I could see was this nightmare of a home. And look what happened to Rachael! Left for weeks in her own excrement—festering away with bedsores. And when she died they sent Robert a bill for two hundred pounds as payment for spirits and chocolates. And Rachel never drank in her life and she was allergic to chocolate.

Lil And *I* would have let that happen to you?

Auntie No—but ... These things happen. Human nature stinks.

Lil Basil's does.

Auntie Look, Lil, I know you've been good to me. And I've been good to you. I know my pension doesn't go far, but I've always freely given it. I've always paid my way.

Lil Auntie, your pension never even paid your weekly bill for cigarettes and gin.

Auntie Oh, that's unkind. That's unkind.

Lil Is it? And what about you? Were you thinking of kindness when you sidled out of the door leaving me crippled with debts, wondering whether to take an overdose or not?

Auntie Lil, don't talk to me like that. Please don't. I'm a sick old woman and I can't take any more of it. And I always loved you, you know that.

Lil And it shows.

Auntie Try and understand—I was frightened. And you said yourself they might repossess the house. All I could see was this nightmare of a home.

Lil But why didn't you talk to me about it? Why run away?

Auntie I didn't—I was going to write and explain.

Lil And when Basil threw you out it was a case of 'the devil you know'. You came back hoping all would be sorted out. And a bit of ironing would make everything in the garden lovely again.

Auntie Lil, I thought of you all the time. And I honestly came back to help. You were always in my prayers.

Lil Yes, well there are times when actions speak louder than prayers.

Auntie And I *will* help. I've got a few savings. It's not much but it all helps.

Lil (*coldly*) A few savings.

Auntie It's a few pounds which might come in handy on a rainy day.

Lil takes a letter out of her suitcase

Lil Yes—well on the last *rainy day* when absence was making your heart grow fonder, *this* (*she thrusts the letter in Auntie's face*) just happened to pop through the letter box.

Auntie (*hand to mouth in fright*) Ooo!

Lil A letter from your bank manager confirming that he'd transferred your *five thousand pounds* to a bank in Kent.

Auntie stares blankly

A few savings. A little bit put aside. Who the hell have you been kidding all these years?

Auntie (*shocked*) I . . . I always said I had a little nest egg.

Lil A little nest egg. Five thousand pounds. And all those years you watched me scratching around—desperately trying to make ends meet. Frantic about where the next penny was coming from. And you were sitting on five thousand pounds.

Auntie I never made any secret of it. I said I had a nest egg.

Lil (*coldly*) Some nest—some egg.

Auntie Lil . . . I can explain . . .

Lil Don't waste your time. I sold virtually everything in this house to pay off those debts and I don't owe a thing. (*She goes to the ironing-board*) And what's left is just not worth bothering about. It's junk. Especially *this*. (*She picks up one of Bill's shirts and rips it to shreds*)

Auntie (*crying*) Stop it! Stop it! You're tearing out my heart.

Leaving

Lil And as far as the house goes—the sooner they repossess it, the better. Then you can see how compassionate your long lost relatives really are.

Auntie In the name of God, Lil, will you stop it. You're going to give me a heart attack.

Lil throws the shirt on the floor and crosses to face the mirror. She leans on the sideboard and tries to compose herself. An awkward silence

(*Quietly*) You can have the money. Just take it.

Lil (*quietly*) I don't want a penny of it. (*Pause*) Did you know he was having an affair with Daisy Parsons?

Auntie No. I wasn't sure. There was talk of someone, but you know what the drama group is like.

Lil You might have warned me.

Auntie I tried to.

Lil Or did you want it to run its course and have him leave. You always did hate him. (*Pause*) Is she pretty?

Auntie Daisy Parsons? She's as ugly as sin. Brash and coarse and as common as muck. I don't know what he sees in her. But then again, he's no better—just a bloody fool.

Lil Sounds as if they were made for each other.

Auntie slowly crosses to pick up the shirt. She gives Lil a long contemptuous look

Auntie (*quietly*) You know Lil, you've made me feel like dirt today. (*Pause*) You share a lot of the blame for our hurt and misery. And hating me won't solve anything.

Lil (*quietly*) I don't hate you, Auntie.

Auntie You were warned not to marry him. Everyone warned you about him but you wouldn't listen. Your mother begged you, pleaded with you—and in the end it sent her to an early grave, I know that.

Lil I married him because I loved him.

Auntie No. You had this obsession about your nose. It was a mania. You thought you were too ugly and you were going to be left on the shelf. So you rushed into marriage with the first man who looked at you twice. And look what he turned out to be—Playboy of the Dole Club—King of the stay-behinds.

Lil It wasn't all bad. It wasn't all his fault.

Auntie You ruined your life because you wouldn't listen to people who gave you good advice. From the day I first met that fool I knew he didn't have a penny to his name. You made the worst of all possible mistakes.

Lil Well . . . this Lily is now gilded. So I'm hardly likely to make the same mistake again.

Auntie You could have had lovely men friends if you'd given yourself a chance. You were refined and cultivated.

Lil Does a bobbed nose and a new gown make me any different?

Auntie You stood out in a crowd.

Lil I certainly did that.

Auntie And you had a good bust and a fine figure. But now . . .

Lil But now what?

Auntie You look like a pensioned-off page three girl.

Lil And *you* think I hate *you*.

Auntie You've sold your mother's jewellery—you've lost all your character—and you've given yourself the bland features of a bingo-caller in a divorced and separated club. Can't you ever do anything right in your life, for God's sake? And you were right about Basil—he did ask me to leave. It was stupid of me to go there thinking I could just walk in and say "Hello I've just popped in to stay for the rest of my life". But after what I'd been through, it was worth a try. But that's life isn't it? You look after people all your life and when you're old and need looking after yourself, no-one wants to know. You're simply regarded as a senile old cow who should have been put down years ago.

Lil All I wanted was the truth.

Auntie Why? You never listened when you were told the truth.

Lil (*shouting*) Oh I listened. I just didn't like what I heard, that's all. And I can still vividly recall how upset you were when I married him. But wasn't that because you wanted this old maid to look after you for the rest of your life? When he appeared on the scene, he was a threat to your cosy future.

Auntie How can you say that? I only wanted the best for you. When you were young your mother and I doted on you. I loved you as if you were my own.

Lil I don't know why—you're not even related to me. You just came from nowhere.

Auntie is extremely upset. She sits on the sofa and buries her head in her hands

Auntie (*sobbing*) All those sacrifices. All that love and care . . . all those years. And I end up being called a parasite. (*Shouting*) You not only look like a tart—you sound like one.

Lil bursts out crying and leans over the arm of the sofa to face Auntie

Lil Auntie . . . please . . . (*Pause*) Just once . . . just this once . . . say something nice to me—make me feel better. Give me something to hope for. Is it too much to ask?
Auntie I used to love that face. To me it will always be my Lil.
Lil (*shouting*) Well, your Lil doesn't exist any more.
Auntie You ask me to give you hope. Well, I can't. Your only hope now will be in a bordello.

Lil storms over to the sideboard. She takes out an old photograph of herself which clearly shows her large nose. She thrusts it in front of Auntie's face

Lil And this? Is this really how you wanted me to look for the rest of my life? Go on, look at it.
Auntie (*crying and turning her head*) Don't Lil, don't. (*Pause*) Please don't.

Lil throws the photograph onto the sofa and walks DL

Lil And you say you loved me?
Auntie Oh God! What's happening to me? What am I going to do? I did love you. I still do. But I can't take any more battering like this—I can't.

Lil slowly turns and walks to the sofa. She sits and stares at Auntie. Another awkward silence

Lil (*quietly*) I'm sorry. (*Pause*) It's not nice is it?—change.
Auntie What's going to happen to me? I don't want to go in a home. Where am I going to end up?
Lil I don't know.
Auntie I only want us to be happy.
Lil Happy. What's happy?
Auntie I'm sorry too. (*Pause*) You only did what you thought was right. I hope it brings you peace of mind. (*Pause*) And you don't look like a tart.
Lil (*genuinely*) Thank you, Auntie.
Auntie You're shaking.

Lil I'm all right.
Auntie Shall I put the heating on?

Lil shakes her head

I could cry when I think of the way that stupid man has ruined our lives. A big, stupid, bloody fool. And he'd no sooner moved in when he bought gnomes for the front garden—showed the sort of mentality he had.
Lil It wasn't all his fault. He tried. In his own way.
Auntie He was a swine.
Lil He wanted children, you see. And I didn't. Well, I did, but I couldn't take the risk.
Auntie The risk?
Lil Of them all looking like that. (*She points to the photograph*)
Auntie (*looking down; wearily*) Oh Lil!
Lil The thought of it horrified me. (*Pause*) And ... he liked to go out for a drink, and why not? But I couldn't. I just couldn't. (*Pause*) There wasn't much give and take on my side either.
Auntie That's all he wanted to do—sup!
Lil Not in the first few years. (*Pause*) And there were good times—it wasn't all bad. And our wedding—it was beautiful.
Auntie In that dingy registry office?
Lil To me it was like St Paul's. (*Pause*) I was so happy. I would have gone to the ends of the earth with him if he'd asked me.
Auntie The incorrigible romantic—a surefire way of becoming one of life's losers. You should have divorced him years ago.
Lil You mean taking the easy way out. I'm not that sort of person. To me marriage was more than just a hobby.
Auntie (*rising*) I'll go and make the tea. Then we can discuss what we're going to do. And that five thousand ... it belongs to both of us. We can ...
Lil Auntie ... before you make the tea ...
Auntie And what good is it to me in the bank? You can't take it with you.
Lil Auntie ... (*Pause*) There is something I have to tell you.
Auntie Oh?
Lil Er ... you'd better sit down.
Auntie (*sitting on the sofa*) What is it?
Lil Auntie ... when I was in London ... I met someone.
Auntie (*devastated*) Oh?

Lil He's ... the sort of man you always wanted me to meet.
Auntie (*quietly; almost losing her voice*) I see.
Lil Educated ... gentle ... compassionate.
Auntie And ... (*cautiously*)—Do you like him?
Lil Yes. Yes I do.
Auntie Does ... he like you?
Lil I think so.
Auntie I see.
Lil I didn't know such men existed.
Auntie I see.
Lil (*half smiling; half tearful*) Oh Auntie ... please stop saying "I see".
Auntie I'm sorry.

Lil clasps Auntie's hands

Lil (*emotionally*) What can I say?
Auntie (*with feigned brightness*) When ... when did you meet him?
Lil Three weeks ago. At an art exhibition.
Auntie Well ... tell me more about him.
Lil You'll meet him anyway. He drove me up from London. He's picking me up at seven.
Auntie Picking you up? So ... you're not staying? You're leaving?
Lil (*quietly*) Yes ... I'm leaving.
Auntie I see. (*Pause*) Lil, would you mind if I had another drink?
Lil (*smiling*) And when did you ever need my permission to have a drink?

Auntie goes to the sideboard to pour another gin and tonic

Auntie Would you like one, Lil?
Lil No thanks. All my life I searched for happiness and never found it. Then I gave up trying and there it was—staring me in the face.
Auntie Is he good-looking?
Lil I think so.
Auntie (*with a feigned laugh*) Any money?
Lil Yes—he's an art dealer.
Auntie Really? Is he married?
Lil No.
Auntie And ... does he know about Bill?
Lil No. He knows nothing about me. And that's the trouble.

Auntie (*sitting on the sofa*) Do you love him?
Lil Oh, Auntie! At my age?
Auntie (*forcing a laugh*) What are you talking about?—at your age. You're still a young woman. You've got a lifetime ahead of you.
Lil Have I?

Pause

Auntie So . . . (*Pause*) Well, well. And er . . . what's his name?
Lil Fred. Fred Graham.
Auntie And . . . does he love you?
Lil Auntie! We've only known each other for three weeks.
Auntie Still, you must have an idea.
Lil He likes me very much.

Auntie rises, desperately trying to hold back her tears. She crosses to above the ironing-board and picks up some of the clothes

Auntie Well . . . (*Pause*) It appears I might have wasted my time on this lot after all.
Lil It was good of you.
Auntie Good? No, it was a reflex action. When you've done it for twenty years it becomes second nature. It was all I could give, you see—a bit of ironing. Not really enough, was it? (*Pause*) Not really enough.
Lil We did our best—in our own fashion. It just didn't work out. (*Pause*) Auntie . . .
Auntie Anyway, it's silly talking about this lot—I should really be wishing you every happiness.
Lil I promised myself I would make a decision this evening.
Auntie About . . . ?
Lil Fred and I—the future—if there is one.
Auntie And have you?
Lil (*rising*) I don't want to cheat him, you see. This morning I passed a building site and they wolf-whistled. Imagine it—men wolf-whistling at me. I walked down that street as if I were on a cloud. Then I realized I would have to tell him that I was eleven years his senior. Tell him that and all the rest.
Auntie D'you have to?
Lil Oh yes. As you said, you can't escape the past.
Auntie If he's the sort of man you say he is then he will

Leaving

understand. It's what you are inside that counts. Let's face it, beauty is only skin deep.
Lil It's all so complicated—too good to be true.
Auntie Then there's me isn't there?
Lil What will you do?
Auntie If you leave me? What anyone would do who's just had her heart ripped out. No. (*Pause*) Ohh, I'll feel very sorry for myself—cry for a few weeks, then . . . try and fall back on my memories. What else can I do?
Lil Auntie . . .

There is the sound of doorchimes

Auntie That must be him.
Lil No, it's too early.
Auntie I'll go.

Auntie exits to the hall

Lil picks up her photograph and stares at it

Auntie returns looking very shaken

Lil, it's Daisy Parsons.
Lil (*coldly*) Really!
Auntie She says she wants to speak to you.
Lil Does she now? Tell her to go to hell.
Auntie But she says it's very important.
Lil What the hell can she want?
Auntie What are you going to do?

Lil thinks for a while

Lil You'd better show her in.
Auntie Aren't you coming?
Lil No, if she wants to talk—she comes to me.
Auntie And don't get drawn into a row. Don't go down to her level.

Auntie exits. She returns followed by Daisy Parsons

In here.
Daisy Thanks. (*She looks at Lil in amazement*) Mrs Smith?
Lil For the present, yes.
Daisy I'm Daisy Parsons.

Lil Really.
Daisy I've got some news about your Bill.
Lil *My* Bill?
Daisy Look, love, I didn't come here for a row.
Lil I most certainly hope you didn't, Miss Parsons—or is it Mrs—nobody seems to know?
Daisy It's Mrs actually, not that it matters. I just want you to know that he's ill.
Lil Really? And why should that concern me?
Daisy You're his wife aren't you?
Lil Now, *that* is rather an academic point at the moment—wouldn't you agree?
Daisy Look, love, I'm a busy woman, I've no time for big words and I've been to a hell of a lot of trouble trying to find you this week. I've called five times and there's been nobody here.
Lil Yes, well I'm sorry to hear of your inconvenience, Mrs Parsons, but if he's ill, what relevance is it to me?
Daisy Look, love ...
Lil And please stop calling me love—coming from you I find it extremely offensive.
Daisy Jees! Are you going to listen to me or not?

There is no reply

Bill is very ill and he needs attention.
Lil Maybe you don't understand. On the second of June, my husband left me a letter in which he stated that he'd fallen for some sort of woman who worked in a tavern and that he was moving up North to start a new life. Now, assuming that approximates to the situation and you are the woman, then I suggest that *you give him the attention!*
Daisy Well, that letter is news to me. It wasn't like that and for your information he's not my scene. It was all a big mistake.
Lil (*sarcastically*) Oh dear!
Daisy Look, he had a stroke and collapsed in a Chinese take-away in Blackpool.
Lil A stroke?
Daisy Yes—a bad one.
Lil So he's in hospital?
Daisy Hospital! He's been in bloody intensive care. They thought

he was going to kick the bucket for two weeks. And we'd only been there a few days when it happened. It certainly put the mockers on my holiday, I can tell you.
Lil A very bad stroke you say?
Daisy Very bad. He's paralysed down one side and he can't talk. But he can understand what you're saying.
Lil (*quietly*) My God!
Daisy They moved him to our local hospital a week ago. There's not much more they can do for him so they want to release him. You can take him today if you want. And I've done enough — I'm up to here with it. He'll need constant attention and, quite frankly, it's just not my problem. I'm sorry, but life's too short.
Lil What ward is he in?
Daisy Ward seven. You can visit him any time.
Lil Does he need anything?
Daisy Not really — he's in good hands. The doctor said in time he may get a bit of his speech back, but ... I don't think he will. He's in a very bad way.
Lil Well, thank you for telling me.
Daisy It wasn't easy — coming here. I know you must hate me but ... I am sorry.
Lil (*quietly*) Are you?
Daisy And that letter ... it wasn't like that, you know.
Lil Well, it's history now, isn't it?
Daisy (*about to go*) Yes ... well ... I've never been a wicked woman — at least I tried not to hurt anyone. But when a fellah offers you the chance of a good time, you don't ask any questions — you grab it, don't you?
Lil Do you?
Daisy You'd be a fool not to. And for what it's worth — he'd have come back to you — I know it. And the way he is now — don't hold it against him. We should all have the right to make a bloody fool of ourselves once in our lives. (*She goes to the hall*) If you can find it in your heart, ring me and tell me how he is. I'll be at the *Crown*.

Daisy exits

Lil walks to the mirror and stares in it

Auntie What are you going to do? (*Pause*) Lil?

Lil continues to stare into the mirror. After a while she turns and slowly picks up her coat

Lil?
Lil I'll walk—it's not far.
Auntie Shall I come?
Lil No.
Auntie Can I do anything?
Lil No.
Auntie How long will you be?
Lil (*going to the hall*) I don't know. I may be late.
Auntie Shall I wait up?
Lil No. (*Pause*) Oh ... there is something you could do.
Auntie Anything. I'll do anything.
Lil (*sighing*) Would you switch on the central heating? And ... could you air his pyjamas ... and his bed clothes?
Auntie Lil?
Lil Hmm?
Auntie What about ... Fred? What shall I say?
Lil Tell him—(*pause*)—tell him I've gone to the hospital.
Auntie To see Bill?
Lil (*quietly*) Yes. Tell him ... tell him everything ... and say I'm sorry.
Auntie But ... ?
Lil And ... (*She goes to the sofa. She picks up her photograph and hands it to Auntie*) ... give him this.
Auntie Is that all?
Lil That's all. (*She returns to the hall*) Oh, and Auntie ...
Auntie Yes?
Lil Thank you for doing the ironing.

Lil exits

Auntie slowly picks up the clothes off the ironing-board. She is deep in thought. Then her mood changes and she replaces the clothes and takes the gin and tonic bottles from the sideboard. She tops up her glass and is about to drink when the telephone rings. She stares at the phone for a while, takes a gulp of gin and lifts the receiver

Auntie (*slowly—coldly*) What—do—you—want? ... Yes, it is ... Hello, Muriel ... I'm well, thank you ... No, I'm afraid you've just missed her ... Oh yes, the play, she did mention it ... The

Leaving

Casting Committee on Thursday. . . . But I thought . . . Eileen's what? . . . She's pregnant! . . . Oh dear . . . Indeed . . . Lil? . . . (*Slowly*) Yes, Muriel, I think she will be available . . . Yes, of course . . . as you say, with subtle make-up and the right lighting . . . Oh, I'm sure she will do it . . . Oh yes, she will do well all right—very well indeed. In fact Muriel, I think you are in for a very big surprise . . . No she's been on holiday, that's all . . . Oh yes, she's back for good . . . Thank you for calling. (*She replaces the receiver, takes another gulp of gin, selects one of Bill's shirts and starts to iron it*)

CURTAIN

FURNITURE AND PROPERTY LIST

On stage: Carpet
Sofa
Coffee table
Armchair
Sideboard. *In it:* glasses, gin, tonic, photograph. *On it:* telephone, piles of mail, ashtray, cigarettes, lighter, glass of gin and tonic
Ironing-board. *On it:* iron, shirt. *By it:* pile of ironed clothes
Mirror
Dressing as desired

Off stage: Clothes to be ironed **(Auntie)**
Suitcase. *In it:* letter. **(Lil)**

LIGHTING PLOT

One interior set. No practical fittings required

No cues

EFFECTS PLOT

Cue 1	As **Auntie** exits to the kitchen *Front door opens and closes*	(Page 1)
Cue 2	**Lil:** "Auntie..." *Doorchimes*	(Page 17)
Cue 3	**Auntie** tops up her glass *Telephone rings*	(Page 20)

www.ingramcontent.com/pod-product-compliance
Lightning Source LLC
Chambersburg PA
CBHW070455050426
42450CB00012B/3295